It Started with Patton

Teresa Leska's Story

A Memoir

Amy E. Zajac

Copyright © 2012 Amy E. Zajac

The photographs are a compilation of collected and assembled material from Teresa Leska's family. This compilation, as used here, refers to the original selection and arrangement of preexisting photographs.

The noted Copyright includes authorship of text, compilation, and editing.

All rights reserved, including the right to reproduce this book or portions of it in any form.

Published by Amy E. Zajac at CreateSpace.

All rights reserved.

ISBN-10: 0988207001

ISBN-13: 978-0-9882070-0-4

In Your Honor, Mom.

Amy

Amy E. Zajac

In Gratitude
My acknowledgment of supportive family and friends.

To my daughters, Sabina Zajac and Teresa Waller, for the hours of conversations supporting every step of the journey to this first book.

To my dearest friend, Polly Morton, for her encouragement and back-up research suggestions, helping me to locate those tidbits that make a difference.

To my friend and fellow writer/author, Donna Sundblad, for her treasured advice and her patience with my unending questions.

To my friend and fellow writer/author, Maureen Pierre, for her encouragement and teaching me to "stay in the moment".

To my friend, Sharon Grimson, for reading and re-reading every new edition giving me her great "reader's" perspective.

CONTENTS

	Introduction	i
1	Spring 1945	1
2	My Life and Family in Poland	7
3	My Life as a Child	12
4	A Friend Remembered	28
5	School	30
6	During the Occupation	33
7	The Villa Next Door	37
8	My Dad and Sabina	39
9	The Last Time with Family	42
10	Sisters Together	45
11	My Life with Strangers	54
12	A Constant	67

13	Leaving Liberated	68
14	When I Met Freddie	70
15	Getting to America	77
16	Finally On Our Own	88
17	Overview	96
18	Jan and Marcianna Leski	98
19	Alfred W. Lejman (Freddie)	102
20	A New Life Again	108
21	My First Trip to Poland	111

INTRODUCTION

For years my sisters and I urged our mother to tell us her early life story in more detail than she ever told us before. Mom described her life to us very generally and stated many times, she thought her life to be "nothing special". She just happened to live in a time of history when the whole world was in turmoil. As she approached her sixties, she finally started to think about her own history a little more. The 50th anniversary of her freedom brought it all into perspective. There was a time when she believed, she would never be living a free life, let alone celebrate a 50th anniversary of her freedom. On the actual anniversary she visited the General Patton Memorial Museum in Chiriaco Summit, California. Seeing so many war artifacts, pictures, and medals honoring, not only General Patton, but all the men who fought so gallantly with him, enlightened the idea that these moments leading to her new life were important. After that, she and I started a process of writing down her story. She talked and gave me what I call snippets of information and always with the caveat, who would want to know this or "Amy I just don't remember". In any case, her story of survival is sad, horrifying, and joyous, filled with more perseverance than any of us ever knew. Self-taught in not only English, but also, every subject we American's need "schooling" for, she is even an award winning quilter, mastering American Quilting to perfection. She reinvented herself over and over, before the term became fashionable.

Her current complete name is Teresa Maria Leska Thomas. However, when she arrived in the United States in 1946, her name was Teresa Maria Leska Lejman. Growing up, her family called her Terenia or Tereńcia, the familiar versions of Teresa in the Polish language. Born in a unique time in the history for Poland, with Germany to the west and the Soviet Union (Russia) to the east, Poland lands were in high demand by both of these bordering countries. During World War II this conflict overtook the Polish people. My mother's perspective comes from a child's memory of the conflict with an adult's rationale.

Amy E. Zajac, Her Daughter

Patton's Third Army

The orders were given; the trek was a prance,

Orders were followed what 'ere consequence.

Forging ahead is all that they did,

The Third Army's glory was just up ahead.

A woman ran crying in front of the charge,

The tanks were so loud, no voices were large.

One soldier jumped down, to be at her side,

He moved her away from a tank in its stride.

They didn't just stand 'round and wait,

They kept on going to liberate,

They gave so many the chance to flee,

To find their families and again be free!

Amy E. Zajac

CHAPTER 1
SPRING 1945

In the spring of 1945, we worked in the potato fields. I dove for a ditch when bullets hit the dirt near me. They sounded like spitting. The dust flew in tiny clouds all in a row. I looked up at the plane, its humming engine whined when it pulled out of the dive taking its place back in formation. The sky, dark with so many planes, shaded us in the fields just like a big cloud floating between the sun and the ground. My guardian angel hard at work saved not only me, but the other forced labor camp workers with me. No one died during this shooting, not even the mean Gestapo guards. I knew the war was not going well for the

Germans. I could tell by the frequency of bombings and with so many Allied airplanes in the sky every day.

Very early in the morning the next day, about 5 a.m., I suspected something unusual was happening. The rumble of tanks on the road could be heard coming in from the west. I didn't know what tanks were, but they were loud and everyone I heard comment about what it was, "something was changing and it was big". The few guards which still remained with us, no longer carried weapons, this added to our speculation. We could always tell when the war went well for the Germans on the warring fronts; the guards were meaner to us. And vice versa, when things went badly for the Germans, the guards were nicer, but, no weapons meant something different altogether. I continued my early morning chores.

At 7 a.m., there were no guards anywhere in sight. If I walked away from the Hartman Farm, the labor camp where I lived for two years near Sehlen, Germany, no one would see me. So…I did. Moments later, when I ran out on the road, at seventeen years of age, I saw my first American tank bearing down quickly toward me. It had a big white star on the front of it. I could not believe my eyes, but…crashing reality hit me. I was free. I stood frozen. The enormous vehicle came closer and closer. It made a loud clackity sound. The soldiers riding on it waved frantically at me, but my legs wouldn't move. One of the men had black skin. I never saw a man with black skin before. He yelled the loudest, but his words were alien. That was the first time I heard English. He waved and waved, almost frenzied, for me to get off the road. In the shock of the moment, I guess, I still didn't move. With the army tank no more than ten feet away, the American jumped off. He literally pushed me to the side of the road. I would have been killed if it wasn't for the tall black man. He jumped right back on the tank, waved and I never saw him again. That was Good Friday, April 3rd, 1945, and I have no memory of the next few hours. I knew one thing. I wanted to find my sister, Lodzia. She should be fairly near, at another farm with displaced person laborers. Being able to make a decision on my own, without anyone stopping me, exploded an odd feeling inside me. I was happy!

With so much turmoil and all the telephone wires torn down by the Allied Forces, communications were very limited. There were no German soldiers anywhere in sight. I thought they were captured and transported as prisoners of war. I found out later the German guards scattered all over the fields. They ran when General Patton's Third Army came through. The Third Army didn't work through the fields in our locale until later.

My driving thought, find my sister. When I got closer to where I thought she would be, about a twelve kilometer walk, I saw German guards carrying pistols and rifles and realized Lodzia was not on Patton's main liberation track. With all the confusion, I feared being captured again by the German's. The only clothes I had clearly showed the big yellow and green letter P, identifying me as Polish. But then…nobody paid any attention! I hid out until Lodzia was freed by finding a small abandoned cabin where I spent the night. Dark, dingy and vacant of furniture, the dilapidated shack sheltered me for the night and from being seen by Gestapo still hiding in the fields. It was very cold and I shivered all night with just my dress, and of course, my horrible wooden shoes.

The next day when I walked to the forced labor farm where I hoped Lodzia was, I saw no German guards anywhere. Like the day before, they had disappeared. I found my way to Lodzia, still on the farm.

She stood in the yard. I knew it was her. I ran over and we hugged. I was shaking all over and didn't want to let go. It had been two years since I last saw her. Patton's Army liberated Lodzia early in the morning that day. She told me she planned to look for me, but it was all so quick; she just hadn't left yet. When we met up again, what a perfect happy moment it was! Blessed freedom!

I stayed in Lodzia's room with her for a few days. It was a regular bedroom in the rooms extended out between the house and workshop, not anything like my cubby in the barn. The owners of the farm where she labored were younger unlike where I worked. They understood we were sisters and said nothing about my staying. I was just glad to be there. Since that part of Germany was then occupied by the western allies, as displaced persons from the conflict, our freedom was secure.

When American military police searched the area for farm laborers, the Bürgermeister in the close by town Sehlen told them we were at the farm. Papers were given to us to fill out and we were told to report to Mönschmille the newly designated camp for displaced persons in our locale. Only a short 5km walk to our first free life experience after two years as prisoners!

General George S. Patton brought me into freedom and my entire life I have appreciated his tenacity. I didn't learn about the Third Army and what a great army officer General Patton was, until much later. I know I'm simplifying and that there are many points of view on his tactics and questionable choices. I go by one fact. What he did gave us freedom again and for that, his memory is honorable and warmly remembered!

CHAPTER 2
MY LIFE AND FAMILY IN POLAND

Born in Sulejów, August 25, 1927, I was the youngest of five children, three girls and two boys. My oldest brother Josef (Joseph) died as a small child, and my brother Mieczysław (Mitchell) died in 1938 in a plane crash. Mieciu, (nickname for Mieczysław) a pilot in the Polish Air Force was an instructor for new recruits. He died in Poznań in front of a large crowd during an air show exhibition. I remember the day of the tragedy very well. I played outside in the warm sunshine when the telegram was delivered. My mother read the piece of paper and then read it again, and again. Her face looked startled like she could not believe what she read, so she kept reading it and then walked away from our house. I followed her because I thought her actions were strange and definitely out of the ordinary. My mother's hands were up in the air; she complained out loud and sobbed all the way to the railway station about 150 feet out the front gate, where she turned around and walked back to our house. When she got home she walked past the house and out through the woods in a circle turning toward our house once again. Mom's erratic behavior made everything feel chaotic and during that chaos, someone went to get my dad at work. In my memory, Lodzia, my eldest sister, appeared at this time and shortly after, Sabina, my other sister, came home. As Sabina always did, she started to cook, to keep busy and put dinner together for everyone. Mieciu was the oldest of all the remaining siblings and none of us could believe he was gone. Devastated by the news, Mom's quiet mood and sullen behavior overshadowed our lives. She struggled to grasp that she'd now lost both her sons. As everyone reminisced about Mieciu, I heard them talk of all his accomplishments and how proud of him they all were. I learned about him in those days, never really grasping all he had done before that. The next couple of days were still chaotic.

Only Dad went to the funeral in Poznań, which was northwest of Sulejów. Because of the economic depression, we couldn't afford to send any other family members. He traveled by train. Once in Poznań, he and Krystyna Szczesna, Mieciu's fiancée, represented our family.

Dad and Krystyna Szczesna follow behind the casket in the funeral procession.

After Mieciu's death, Mom went outside many times, and stared at the sky for hours. He had been stationed at the Ławica Air Force Base near Poznań, about 200 Km away and periodically flew over our town, tipping his wings so we knew it was him. Mom suffered terribly by this loss of a son for the second time.

Except for my brother's death, the years leading up to that point were good memories for me. My dad worked in a saw-mill, operating large steam machinery as a lead, which produced the power for driving all the machines. My mother, mostly at home with her children, did work part-time to help make ends meet. She purchased vegetables at local farmers markets, and delivered the vegetables for sale to a sanatorium for people with tuberculosis.

Sulejów, which means Saltville, the town of my birth, got its name from merchants who used the Pilica River for transportation of salt from the mines in the south of Poland. My oldest sister, Lodzia, told me this story and I thought of it almost like a fairy tale.

Sulejów was a stopover for the barges shipping salt and watching them float along the river fascinated me. I daydreamed about where they traveled to and the adventures of the people who traveled on board. It's one of the good memories from my childhood, which I learned at about age ten.

A memorable part of my life as a child were my animal friends, Kizia, my kitty and, Kozka, the goat I got about one year before the war. Not really understanding why my mother arranged it at first, Kozka was bred to have a baby goat. We would then have a second Kozka. (Kozka means little goat and I always named my goats the same, just like I always named my cats, Kizia, which means kitty.) My mother knew that when the war started, they wouldn't have milk from cows, so having goats that were lactating would help to provide milk for me, twelve years old and still growing.

CHAPTER 3
MY LIFE AS A CHILD

Since my family lived right on the banks of the Pilica River, we were directly across from the Cistercians Monastery. The thousand year old ruin was my playground and served as a background for our daily living. I used my kayak to get across the river to meet my chums, where we played hide and seek in some of the partial buildings still standing. We moved into that house in 1935 and life was good. As time wore on, adults who spoke about the war more and more scared me and my friends. I heard new words in daily conversations, like bombs, poison gas, Nazis and Gestapo. With those words, they spoke about horrible things that were going to happen to everyone.

Our home looked like a single level house from the front, but opened up to multiple levels on the back side by the river, where my bedroom was on the second floor. The fence and the gate in the front were shared by the doctor's villa next door. A large glassed in porch across the front of the house sat behind birch trees scattered all around. The yard was mostly sandy with interspersed bits of grass. I never remembered the grass being mowed and we had a very tall dark brown shiny ceramic planter on the front steps where lavender pinkish peonies draped heavily over the sides every spring.

The back yard had huge weeping willows which extended out over the banks of the river, where I played with my friends, climbing up, swinging out and dropping into the water.

About twenty to thirty feet to the garden from the willow trees was a concrete stone wall which kept the water out when the river rose in the rainy season. This flooding only happened occasionally, but we all knew why the walls were there. In the corner of the yard was the well, with the hand crank. In the garden there was a large veranda which was separate from the house, like a gazebo. Every year it overgrew with scores of grape vines creating a natural umbrella to shade from the extreme heat of summer.

Down the road and around the corner the city cemetery lay quiet behind a humble rock wall. With easy access on our walk from school every day, my best friend, Janina Serafinówna and I, usually stopped to talk and play. Many evenings we played in the cemetery and after dark ran home to get away from the haunting ghosts, a happy memory from so long ago.

During the summers of my eighth, ninth and tenth year, the resorts and rentals along the river filled with tourists from the cities. When many of the same families returned year-after-year, I enjoyed friendship with the "summer" children. My dad built a large stage out of sand in the garden during those years and placed a rope between two of the willow trees, where blankets hung as curtains for the stage. My friends and

I put on plays for our parents and families, creating quite elaborate shows with costumes and props we'd put together all by ourselves. These summer memories stand out in my mind, even after more than seventy years.

Late one night as my family all slept, the house filled with carbon-monoxide gas when someone accidentally closed the flue on the pot belly type stove in the kitchen. The old heater connected to only one other room in the house, my very large bedroom, which I shared with my sisters. I went to bed early and I was sound asleep when my sisters came in later. Soon the quiet house with all of us sleeping was disrupted by my waking up. First I choked when I threw up in my sleep. Mom and Dad woke when they heard me choking as I got sicker and sicker. My sisters, too, started to wake from the noise, especially when our parents woke to help me. Sabina and Lodzia would stir, but could not stay awake. When our parents couldn't keep the older girls up, they opened the windows, but struggled and couldn't get all of us out of the house by themselves. My dad rushed to our neighbors for help and one of them ran to the train station close by, where there was a telegraph. Word was sent a short distance to the emergency center at the hospital in Piortkow Trybunalski fifteen kilometers away. Very soon after that an ambulance vehicle arrived. The medics transported my sisters out of the house and flung them into the snow, hoping to wake them from their unnatural slumbers. They pumped their stomachs and resuscitated them and gave them oxygen. All survived this incident, and all were grateful that I woke so drastically sick. My family attributed all our survival to the fact that I woke up vomiting unlike the rest of the family who didn't awaken, but just slept on. All our lives were saved.

A Girl Scout for several years before the war, I loved all activities with my troop. I was my Patrol's Leader, where we worked on badges together. In many challenges, my Patrol usually achieved first place, a fact I was very proud of, except for one very memorable occasion. A swimming badge challenge, to watch out for our friends within the patrol while swimming, should have easily been another first place achievement. I loved anything involved with swimming and being in the water. The moment deteriorated when we started to splash each other, and began swimming in wrong directions and just plain giggled our way into a free-for-all! We didn't follow any of the rules and received a zero for the challenge.

In the summer of 1939, my sisters prepared the house for "what was to come". They taped the windows, so they wouldn't shatter. They also covered them with multiple layers of paper, so light would not show through at night in case of bombing. The Germans were progressing across Europe, country after country, claiming lands as part of their German Reich Protectorate. Poland stood its ground against the aggression. The Germans attacked through a ground assault from the west side of Poland. After six to seven weeks of fighting, Poland capitulated. The occupation of Poland started. We were no longer free people. This action should have taken longer than it actually did, but since the Russians attacked Poland from the east, the end came fast. The help promised from our allies in "the west", never came. What a blow. Aware of these things even as a child, I was afraid. My world changed.

Concerned about what she heard through conversations with neighbors, Mom knew that certain items would disappear from the store shelves right away. In one of the earliest days of September, she sent me to the store to get sugar and salt. I remember waiting in line listening to some women talk about the war.

The women said the bombs would spread poison particles like rain drops, and they would eat away at our skin and then our skin would fall off our bodies. My imagination went crazy thinking about the bombs falling and what they would do. I was petrified…and suddenly someone was pouring water over my face. The women in the store knew me and quickly went to get my mother. Lodzia and Mom ran to the store and when I came to, I was in my mother's arms. Even though I knew I was okay, everyone else was very concerned because they didn't understand why I fainted. This was the first time I ever fainted, but it wouldn't be the last.

My father decided to send me "home" with his mother, who was visiting us for the summer. He sent word to the farm and the next day, his brother Josef, who lived on the farm with their mother, arrived with a horse drawn wagon. Normally, I liked visiting the old homestead, but this time I would be going without my family. Everyone kissed and said good-bye to me, as if they would never see me again. My grandmother, Uncle Josef and I rode in the wagon to the old farm house in a very remote village, fifteen kilometers away.

I didn't know how close I came to not seeing my family again, because on the third of September, Sulejów was attacked by Germany. I guessed that the Germans worked to wipe out the bridges and the railroad in Sulejów. I stood and watched on the hill at the top of the meadow with my grandmother and Uncle Josef. There was a very large fire. We watched the billows of smoke in the distance and knew bombs were exploding. Because I didn't see close enough to know for sure, I accepted what I heard from my uncle and grandmother. They could tell it was big---Sulejów was probably destroyed. This destruction meant possible fatalities for my family.

Ten days later, I was in the house looking out the window toward the meadow up the hill. In the distance, I saw three people appear over the rise. At first they were so far away, I didn't know who they were. Then, I recognized Mom. I tore out the door and raced up the hill running as fast as my little legs would take me. She, Lodzia and Sabina also broke into a run when they saw me chasing toward them. I couldn't believe my eyes; I was so happy. We all hugged and cried and held onto each other for a long time. Sabina and Lodzia hardly spoke. They acted very protective toward me, touching my face and holding onto my shoulders and just let Mom talk. They didn't want to scare me by saying the wrong things. Mom explained that the main bridge out of town was bombed. They borrowed a little boat to cross the river so they could come to see me. When I didn't see Dad with them, my first questions were about him. Mom quietly said, "Your dad stayed behind to protect our property."

While having dinner that evening, I learned more about what Mom meant about our property when she explained to my grandmother and Uncle Josef. "One bomb fell in the garden very close to our house, but luckily the house withstood the explosion. All the windows shattered along with anything breakable, like dishes, glassware and framed pictures." Prior to the bombings, they buried everything in the ground which still had value, like the Singer Sewing Machine recently purchased for my sister, Lodzia.

When the bombs stopped and after Sulejów was destroyed, the revulsion they experienced pushed Mom and my sisters to come visit me. They only brought a few belongings and were all extremely upset because of what they witnessed. Somehow they acted different to me, especially Sabina, because she used to be so upbeat and happy. Now she barely spoke and frowned, as if she was deeply troubled.

A few days later Mom walked back home, because she was so worried about Dad. She carried a big bag of potatoes and a loaf of bread, just baked by my Aunt Hania, Uncle Josef's wife. Mom knew food would be needed once she got home. She left the three of us with our grandmother and Uncle Josef.

Both Lodzia and Sabina, affected very strongly by the tragedy they saw in Sulejów, transformed their anxiety into action. The Germans made them fearful for their safety and promoted a tremendous need to stay free. Out behind the barn on the back side of our grandmother's property, just past the stream where the cows gathered to drink every day, there was a very dense forest.

Lodzia and Sabina gathered hand tools like, shears, saws, and shovels. They set to work to burrow out a cave-hiding-place for themselves within the denseness of the blackberry vines grown into a solid mass after many years. Literally creating a home for the three of us to hide away and sleep in every night, so they could be confident we were safe from harm or capture. I didn't help much, or at all, with this endeavor; I was off playing and enjoying the farm, happy my sisters were so close by.

My grandmother and Uncle Josef laughed at Lodzia and Sabina. They didn't understand why they would do such a crazy thing. Having not been to Sulejów, to see the destruction and huge loss of life, their perspective remained different.

Four weeks passed without any word from my parents. The German forces took over Poland totally during that time. People shared information by word-of-mouth or they learned from sporadic radio transmissions about the progress of the war. We heard the occupation settled down a bit and that no one was able to move around freely in the cities, and also very noticeable, there were fewer and fewer bombings. Sabina and Lodzia, concerned about our parents, decided it was time to go back home to help. I tried to convince them to take me home with them, because I missed Mom and Dad and I needed to look for my cat and my goat. They held their ground, knowing that Dad would be very cross, if they didn't follow his instructions about my staying at the farm. They refused my pleas and left me behind.

Uncle Josef worked the farm and started to harvest potatoes. He and others dug up the potatoes, and let them lie on the ground. He directed me and several other people to walk along with a small cart and pick them up placing the potatoes into the cart. I didn't like doing it, because it was work. I wanted to play, as young twelve year old girls do. I spoke to Uncle Josef about how I wanted to go home; he thought I should want to stay, so I could help them with the harvest. I understood that he couldn't think about the little girl I was, and how I didn't want to work in the fields and that I missed my parents and sisters. After about a week of working with the potatoes, I decided to go home. I just walked away and didn't say anything to anyone on the farm. I started out early one morning. No one bothered me as I walked through the countryside. I walked through fields and stayed away from the main roads. It took me all day to walk the 15 kilometers; I arrived at dusk, just light enough to be able to see my way. When I arrived in Sulejów, what I saw was a nightmare. I heard adults talking as I walked. They said that of the ten thousand residents of Sulejów, half of them died. I saw dead bodies everywhere. Seeing pieces of bodies made me gag, and my stomach was upset. The nauseous feeling made me very uncomfortable, because everything smelled so horrible. No bodies were buried or picked up because there wasn't anyone to do it at that point yet. It took a lot of time for this to get accomplished. I couldn't wait to get home, my fear felt oppressive. I wanted my parents.

When I arrived they were happy to see me, and yet not happy to see me. My dad wanted me to stay on the farm for a month or two more; I saw in his face the added burden I created. They didn't want me to see the destruction and the dead bodies that I encountered on my way home. My life on the farm would have remained "normal" for an extended period of time, because food and a regular life situation still existed so far from Sulejów. So sure that my parents would be glad to see me, I didn't understand why they expressed anger, but after a while, I realized it wasn't about me. They just wanted me "to be safer on the farm".

I poked around to see the changes and the destruction on our property. The house was already fixed up a little. All the windows were boarded up. The mark of the closest bomb destroyed my favorite willow tree which I played under my whole life. In its place…a huge hole.

Kozka was tied up at the back of the house and I was so glad to see her again, but I never found Kizia. I was sad at her loss, but eventually I found some kittens who once again became my little Kizia's.

During my first moments of discovery in Sulejów, I also experienced, for the first time, seeing how terrible the German Gestapo and SS treated the people still alive. The German soldiers were everywhere; some were arresting people, others hit and kicked survivors, and when they fell bleeding, they would laugh at them like it was a party. I appeared to be invisible to them. They did not pay any attention to kids like me.

I did not expect it to be so different just to live. There were five to six families living with us, as those families lost their homes completely. This was a real shock. Someone else lived in my bedroom.

CHAPTER 4
A FRIEND REMEMBERED

After the occupation stabilized, finding food involved everyone, and became our highest priority. One day Mom sent me to buy bread. Several houses scattered throughout the area had large ovens that were partially outside. When black market flour became available, the families baked bread for sale. Mom heard from a neighbor about the baking and sent me right away to buy a loaf. Getting there early was key to getting a loaf and that time I made it just right. I paid with the "occupation money" Mom gave me.

On my way home, just after passing the city

hall steps and enjoying the aroma and the warmth of the newly baked bread, I looked back when I heard loud voices and the commotion of people pushing each other with loud shuffling feet. The young priest from my church, being taunted by Gestapo, fell on the steps. Before he could even try to stand up, a Gestapo drew his luger from his belt and shot him in the back and as if just by a reflex replaced the luger back in his belt when he finished. Horrified and unable to catch my breath, I held tight to my bread, turned and ran. I felt odd, and somehow disoriented, and I didn't stop until I got home. Mom held me close, "Take a deep breath, Tereńcia." I tried to breathe calm enough to express my fear and tell her what I saw. When Daddy got home later that evening, I told him, too. My parents spoke very hopeful; telling me he may be okay, but after that I never saw him again. No one ever spoke of him. It was almost like he was never even there in the first place.

CHAPTER 5
SCHOOL

The winter of 1939 thru 1940, the Germans decided to reopen our schools. Their intent was for us Polish children to learn the German language. Some teachers already knew a little German; however, it was hard for everyone. I didn't like it at all, and even though I didn't want to, I learned German anyway.

My homeroom teacher, Helena Samborska, who should have been my teacher through seven years of schooling, didn't come back when school reopened that year. She disappeared along with many other teachers and important town's people. I never saw or heard of her again.

Teresa is the fourth from the right in the bottom row. Her lost teacher, Helena Samborska, is in the center of the picture.

The missing people were never accepted, but after a while it was a normal thing. Everyone became conditioned to unusual things which started to become part of our daily lives.

While I learned German in school, my father and my sisters, Lodzia and Sabina, worked with the underground resistance forces. (Many years later I learned they all went by pseudonyms while supporting the underground activities; they called my dad, Dziadek, meaning old granddad, they called Lodzia, Szyszka, which meant Pine Cone and they called Sabina, Sarna, which meant Deer.)

Lodzia worked hard with the resistance activities, while I grumbled about going to school to learn German. She became friends with others working in the resistance movement from different locales when they would assist each other in so many different ways. She fell in love during that time and planned to be married. Sadly, as I remember only a little, there was talk about a small family wedding which never occurred. He never returned from a secret trip. I just knew after a while no one talked about the wedding anymore. Lodzia found out later that he had been killed during this secret trip for the resistance movement. His loss changed her life forever.

CHAPTER 6
DURING THE OCCUPATION

Underground communications and contacts were made through our house in Sulejów. So near the river and at the edge of town, the strategic location of our house made it a logical place to work through. Much information was passed back and forth for the Polish government people in exile in England. A "safe house" for downed pilots, people in transit, and simply anyone who attempted to hide from the Germans in so many different circumstances. They came through, and stayed usually at night after I was already in bed. Even though I knew someone stayed with us overnight, they were already gone in the morning, by the time I got up. I heard voices in the house; that was all. However, on one occasion, the door was open and I saw three men. They spoke Polish. During the couple moments I saw through the door, my dad handed them guns and identification cards. I believed they were pilots who were in the Polish division of England's Royal Air Force. When I saw this, I was not scared or surprised. It was simply part of my life at the time. Dad kept equipment for the resistance locked up in a storage room in the cellar. I don't remember ever going into that room.

Throughout the four years occupation, while the Gestapo and SS controlled our lives, inside I felt as if I did something wrong, my parents could not protect me from anything and that I didn't belong to

Mom and Dad anymore. The SS and Gestapo always close by, the horrible sound in my ears with their stomping boots intimidating everyone.

The Germans needed our country to continue with our farming, harvesting, and running our mills, so their soldiers would have food and all their other needs met on a regular basis. A veterinarian assigned to work in the locale by the river, came to live in two of the rooms upstairs in my family's house. He brought his new wife with him. Married the day before they arrived, when they came to the door the newlyweds held their hands up, both so excited, they showed our family their new wedding rings. The vet set up his clinic, without an actual office. When he treated an animal, it would be outside in our yard. My friends and I watched as each animal came and went. One day a woman brought her cow that was pregnant and ready to give birth. The vet told the woman that it was going to be a breech birth. When I heard him say this, I didn't know what it meant. He went on to explain that he would help the calf to be born the best that he could. I was fascinated, and watched along with my friends, how the vet helped. He greased both of his arms all the way up to his shoulders, probably with Vaseline, and reached inside the cow to move and force the calf's legs into a position so he could pull the calf slowly into its new life. I couldn't believe my eyes. This beautiful calf was suddenly right there in front of me. At first it struggled to breathe and the vet wiped its face off and blew into its nose and mouth. When it caught its first breath, I took a deep breath, too. Having the calf survive gave us all an uplifted feeling and we were happy to watch the woman pull the cow by the rope to go home with the new calf following close behind. My friends and I were glad this happened during the day, so we could be outside to watch. It made us feel that our lives had a little normalcy. With the curfew in force, no one was allowed out after dark for any reason.

CHAPTER 7
THE VILLA NEXT DOOR

The house next door to ours, a very large and beautiful villa, belonged to Dr. Władysław Kwapiński. The SS occupied the villa using it as a command post after they arrested the doctor and his two sons, who were also doctors. SS officers housed there in comfortable living quarters held elaborate parties on a regular basis. Being a child, I really didn't understand the irony of the activities of the underground resistance filtering through my own house right next door to a German headquarters station. We were under a curfew all the time, and we didn't dare break the restriction, especially since the worst of the

German military, the SS, were so close by.

From approximately September 1939 to the spring of 1941, during the summer and through the fall months when windows were opened for extended periods of time, beautiful music came from the villa so close by. The sweet tones drifted through the trees landing in my ears like they came from an angel's harp. My mother explained to me, "It sounded like someone is playing a zither", since there were no record players or radio during that time. In my mind I could not imagine that a "mean" person like an SS soldier could play such angelic music and then the next day, this same person, is out within the group of the usual six SS men, with their loud shoes, killing people for no cause.

CHAPTER 8
MY DAD AND SABINA

After four years of leading successful local resistance activities through our house, the Gestapo came in force to arrest Dad. One of our neighbors told the Gestapo about what he saw going on at our house aiding so many people in flight from the Germans, plus I learned years later that Lodzia and Sabina helped two downed allied pilots get to safety around that same time. One of these men was shot later and the other captured and tortured. During the torture he may have given my dad's and sister's names to the Gestapo torturers, at least this is a theory, reinforcing the Gestapo logic for seeking out my dad.

Our neighbor came with the Gestapo to find Dad. He was of German decent and my interpretation of what happened, he acted as a spy for them. There were many people who did this type of spying for favors from the Germans. When they didn't find Dad at home, the German neighbor told the Gestapo, "Their father must be at work." Since Sulejów had multiple saw-mill plants, and my dad worked as an electrician at more than one of them, the Germans didn't know which saw-mill to go to. It took them a little time to figure it out. Another neighbor saw the Gestapo at our house and ran to tell Sabina, who was at work. After being told that the Germans were searching the mills, Sabina warned Dad. By the time the Gestapo got to the correct saw-mill, my dad was already gone. He went to hide with the resistance forces. We heard later that our German neighbor recognized Sabina as she walked back to the bakery where she worked. He said, "That's his daughter, she must have told him we were on our way, that's why he escaped". With his accusation, the Gestapo grabbed Sabina off the street and took her away. No one in the family knew she was taken. She didn't come home that night, nor the next day. "Sabina was just gone." There were no goodbyes, no hugs, and no expressions of hope. (She was in jail in Piortkow Trybunalski, a nearby town being interrogated. After a week, they sent her to Auschwitz where she spent the rest of the war. I learned many years later about Sabina's experience. She described it as, "hell on Earth".)

Teresa and Sabina

1943

CHAPTER 9
THE LAST TIME WITH FAMILY

Mom, Lodzia with her son, Jurek, and I all lived in terror of the Gestapo and the SS. Sabina vanished and we knew because there was no message from her, she wasn't hiding with the resistance groups. We stayed close together in the house, I was scared all the time, and I could tell everyone else looked and acted scared, too. My Aunt Mary, mom's sister, moved in with us during that time. What would be next? It never occurred to us that it would be so soon, the horror came only three weeks after Sabina disappeared.

The large and thunderous Gestapo took over our life in a split second. Mom's face was frantic and alarming. She and Aunt Mary followed Lodzia and me to the train station. It was all so rushed, and agitated and loud, but they followed close behind us anyway. I cried and every movement threatened me. I tugged at Lodzia and became clingy. Mom and Aunt Mary stood as close as they could at the train station. Still not allowed to say goodbye, I held her quick loving words back at the house in my mind, when we took a few minutes to gather some belongings. Even though it was scary and loud with the Germans in the house yelling for us to hurry, Mom grabbed a quick hug. The memory of the fear in her eyes scared me. Mom couldn't keep me safe. She said, "Listen and do what authorities tell you to do."

When the train pulled away, the Gestapo shoved and kicked her. She stumbled and fell to the ground when she tried to reach us and touch us one last time. That was the last memory I had of her; I did not see her again for twenty three years.

(I learned many years later that Sabina did not tell the Germans anything about Dad's activities with the resistance.) After three weeks of her horrible interrogation, in the month of March, the Gestapo came to the house and took Lodzia and me away. The Germans thought by taking us too, Dad would come out of hiding. The worst day of my life holds only specific memories.

CHAPTER 10
SISTERS TOGETHER

At first, we didn't know where we were being taken. We boarded a regular train car with seats in it, leaving from Sulejów; however, we stood. All the seats were full. A large group of people were taken from Sulejów that day. We knew the Germans took this many people away almost every day. Most people were taken to western parts of Germany to work as prisoners in many different job functions. But we heard guards talking that this particular day, our train was taking us to Kassel, near the Ruhr Valley, an industrial section of Germany, where we would work in munitions factories. After only a short time we arrived in Piortkow Trybunalski, a close-by town, and transferred to the next train. The cars in this train had no seats like the first train; people sat on boxes or wood shelf-like benches around the outside wall of the boxcar. In the rest of the car people stood or sat on the floor as the transport continued onward to Vienna the next planned stop. I believed this type of train was usually used to transport military people. The route through southern Poland took us over railway tracks not so disrupted by bombings, like in the north, and took only eighteen hours. Bombings weren't directed at the beautiful city of Vienna, just all around it. My guardian angel got us through those bombings. We arrived at the large Vienna train yard.

The damaged tracks on the outskirts of Vienna delayed the next leg of our transport. The Gestapo took all of us from our train to a warehouse to be housed and to sleep. Every day we marched back to the train. Held there just waiting for the train to leave, the long day holds no memory for me, but when the train didn't leave we were once again taken back to the warehouse. This happened over and over again for five days. During those five days, the Gestapo separated the men and women, had them strip down to take community-type showers, within the warehouse, to be de-liced. Being one of the youngest in the large group, my emotional discomfort being with many older women, pregnant women, and the gawking Gestapo guards caused anxiety and embarrassment I never experienced before. I suffered through the shame of this event several times. Lodzia and I learned quickly that after the shower, we could grab a place for the night on the huge area of wood-slats raised above the floor to sleep. I dressed very fast before I was even dry and laid down on the edge of the wood and held tight to keep my place; Lodzia did the same. I was so small and had so little strength; it was so much better to be at the edge, and not have other people almost smother me as I tried to sleep.

One of the nights as I clutched tight to the wood edge, I focused on something a short distance away on the floor. It was a black line moving across right in front of me. The line traveled parallel to me and when I leaned over to look closer, the line turned toward me. The line was hundreds of lice all following in a row. When I realized what they were, I reached out and brushed them away with my hand. That quick action only held them off for a short time. I woke the next morning scratching my neck and my arms; the lice found me after all. I never had lice before that time.

Once the railway tracks were fixed, we were placed on a cattle car train. It held many people all standing in each car. Straw on the floor collected human waste and smelled horrid. The guards called us animals, because everyone was dirty from traveling in the filthy train cars. We moved west and farther and farther from Poland for five to six weeks. The train stopped many times when it came upon heavily bombed out tracks. Waiting for repairs took a lot of time. During these unscheduled stops, shoveling out the cattle cars and spreading new straw, handled by prisoners with that as their specific job, occurred once in a while. I was grateful for the clean-up; the stench of human waste permeated every breath I took.

When the train stopped and the Gestapo opened the doors, people would go off in every direction, eager to get fresh air and space. One time a Gestapo guard yelled at me to stop when I walked in the wrong direction away from the train car. He wanted me to come back toward the train with the other people. When I didn't hear him and do it right away, he caught up to me and hit me across the face with the handle of his luger pistol. Five of my teeth broke and I fell to the ground. Lodzia, horrified at the sight of me being brutalized, had no way to protect me. It was at that moment I told myself I would never do anything to let myself be hit again. I would remember the horrible pain. With no medical treatment for the injury, I suffered terribly long-term with broken teeth and a broken jaw.

During that transport along our train route when it was time to eat, huge kettles of cabbage in water for everyone were set out at our planned stops. I was grateful to be out in the fresh air, but I didn't like the food, I was a very finicky eater. After a while Lodzia, frustrated with me not eating, finally said, "Eat or you're going to die. This is all we've got." I got the message and started eating. Getting food from the top of the kettle was hard. I was so little that I was pushed out of the way many times. The scoops of food near the bottom of the kettle were always full of gravelly dirt and tasted horrible. I knew that something that tasted that dreadful could not have any food value like near the top where the vegetable floated in the broth. Most other memories from this journey of horror, I've blocked out, as if the images first in my mind were wiped clean. I believe this allowed me to survive day-to-day through the many weeks of transit and through the degradation and loss of my childhood.

After a while, the train stopped in a town. I'm not sure, but I believed it to be Frankenberg. When transport trains like the one we were on came through the area with prisoners, it made periodic stops even though there was no damage to the tracks. The local farmers came and picked out some people from the groups of prisoners to work on their farms. That day there was only one farmer who needed five people. Some would work for him and others would work for other farmers in that locale. I felt relief to be outside the cattle car, but the relief, quickly overshadowed by the cruel guards, only lasted a few minutes. The soldier guards lined all of us up for inspection by the farmer who proceeded to make his choices. He chose Lodzia, seven years older than me, as one of the five. He didn't even notice me. So little, only 14 ½ years old at the time, I probably didn't look like I would be good for hard work. The soldiers started yelling that it was time to get back onto the train, "Hurry and finish." It was then that Lodzia boldly stated in a very loud voice, "but if you separate us, we will never see each other again". I panicked and started to cry when I heard my sister speak. Lodzia then said in a few broken German words that, "we are sisters". The farmer looked at Lodzia and then back at me, and walked away, but he stopped, when she said one more word to him…"PLEASE".

At that same time, the Gestapo again yelled, "hurry, the train has to leave". The farmer said, "Well alright" and that's how Lodzia and I came to be taken to the labor camps and worked on the farms, instead of to Kassel to work in the munitions factories. I believed our guardian angel watched over us again that day. Even though this occurred and it was good, we were still prisoners. At least we were not anywhere near the constant bombings, which made daily life extremely fearful in Kassel.

The farmer loaded the six of us onto a wagon pulled by two large black horses. We sat in straw. The high wagon sides only allowed us to see where we past, not what came ahead of us. The wagon stopped at the first farm. As instructed by the farmer that chose us, I gathered up into my arms my scarf, a dress and a heavy jacket that Lodzia took from our suitcase and I stepped off. The driver said, "You'll be told where your sister is later." I couldn't even say good-bye to her, a soldier just kept saying to "hurry up and get out".

Another farmer waited at the side of the road. He towered over me as I looked up at him. "Now what am I supposed to do with you, you're just a little kid?" My German lessons paid off; I understood him.

As I stared up at the man, the wagon abruptly pulled away when the horses started into a gallop, breaking my connection to the giant in front me. I watched and frantically waved, crying as the wagon turned the bend and Lodzia was gone!

CHAPTER 11
MY LIFE WITH STRANGERS

With necessary harvesting to get accomplished in Germany, the use of slave labor which was established prior to the occupation in Poland, was used. At the farm with the giant man, the house, my final destination in the small town of Sehlen, had big beams of wood in its ceilings. It was two stories high, and half of the house was collapsing. People called it the Hartman house and the family had six brothers. Some of the brothers were SS. The one brother, the giant man who met me at the wagon and worked the farm, acted as if he was a good and nice man, but even with that, I was afraid to tell him where I was from. I called him Hartman, never anything else. I didn't say Mr. Hartman and I never knew his first name. This made it simple. I really didn't know him. I didn't talk about myself to anyone on the farm. I feared for my family and what the SS could do to them back in Sulejów, even though I didn't even know if anyone was there anymore.

There was a very old woman living at the farm; I called her Umma which meant granny and actually she was the grandmother in the Hartman family and she wore very old-fashioned clothing. I only saw pictures in school books of pioneers who wore that type of clothing. No one wore clothing like those in my home town or even back at the homestead where my grandmother and uncle's family lived an old fashioned simple life. (When I think back, my remembrance of her was simple. She reminded me of the witch in the Wizard of Oz movie I saw much later after coming to the states.)

I didn't understand why the Hartman house was so dilapidated. Over time, I learned that before the war started, they were going to rebuild the old house, but when the war progressed, the Hartman's were not allowed to do anything like that. They had to wait until the house completely fell apart. I was taught how to mix stucco, put together with straw to help repair and maintain the creaking old building.

At first, I stayed in a barracks with about thirty to thirty-five people. I didn't ask anyone about their life or why they were there, just like other prisoners never asked me either. No one spoke about their personal circumstances. With this consistent pattern, the longer time went on, we didn't take a chance to get to know each other; the idea of trust just died. People become submissive. No one had pride in themselves or what they did or had the ability to say "no" to anything or anyone. I didn't allow myself to cry. If I cried every day, I would not have learned to take care of myself.

Daily we were taken to the different farms around the area. I ate a big meal with them at the end of every work day, usually rutabaga or cabbage soup with bread. For lunch at the farm I was given a slice of meat and a piece of bread. After a while I wasn't around the other people at the barracks, I stayed at the Hartman farm all the time. I don't remember why that changed.

At night I curled up in my blanket, filled with my loneliness, trying to see Mom's face and feel her hug, wondering if my Dad was alive. A little window with a hook to keep it closed could be swung open over the sloping roof, but mostly I blocked the musty mildew smell by seeing Mom bake baba bread in my mind's eye, remembering the familiar aroma of the yeast bread drifting around my head. Those nights alone in the dingy cubby hole at the back of the farmhouse above the stored potatoes and kohlrabi, trapped me in endlessness. And only sometimes tears drenched the blanket when I got lost in the sorrow of missing my family. Will I ever see them again? Where are they? Are they alive? What happened to Sabina? Did Lodzia remember where I was? The stifling small space encompassing my sadness with only enough space for a mattress, a pillow, and blanket, with only a sliding brace on the broken door, was where I learned to fall asleep in my family daydreams. The pain in my jaw, once in a while still cut into my reminiscences. Morning loomed ahead and I knew I would be expected to be at work early, sleep or no sleep.

Once I stayed at the farm all the time, I heard bells ringing every Sunday. It was always right at noontime. When I asked, Hartman told me the bells were at the Catholic Church in the nearby village of Haina. After that I looked forward to hearing the bells, a reminder of home so far away.

Another worker, Jella, came to the farm, but she got better quarters than I had, because she was Ukrainian and only there through a volunteer program. Although, Hartman, the farmer, treated Jella the same as me, she didn't always work in the fields; she spent time as housekeeper. She also had a room in the house so different than my cubby hole. Jella and I became friendly after a period of time. We both understood enough of the other's language that we were able to get along.

I kept hope, because I thought I knew where they took Lodzia. I tried a few times to sneak away at night to see if I could find her. This plan never worked for me though.

Around the farm, the Gestapo security loomed. They were older men and led the people back and forth from the barracks and then stayed at the farm throughout the day. As time went by, mostly they were just "gone", with just a few of them around here and there. For me it was better. I knew I couldn't leave. I had nowhere to go and I knew I could take care of myself. Later, I heard these security Gestapo, were placed with the regular German army to back up the dwindling Nazi military. They handled jobs like logistics and worked as supply clerks.

My listed jobs were many. I milked cows, cleaned out the barns, learned how to kill a goose hanging it up-side-down and cutting its head with a knife, cleaned out horse and cow stalls, scraped out a ditch and placed the dirt in a wheel barrow and layered it with straw to build manure for use in the spring for planting. I wrapped my feet in burlap while working in the ditches and in the barn, because the wooden shoes absorbed the cow's urine and moisture from the feces. In the winter, I liked this job the best. When I stepped onto the filthy barn floor, the steaming manure warmed my feet in the cold and gave me great comfort. The stench didn't matter, because my feet stopped hurting from wearing the wooden shoes. The shoes given to me as I grew out of my shoes from home had wooden soles, with a heel carved in. The winter shoes had higher sides which I laced up a short way. In the summer time I wore just the straight flat wood sole with a strap over the top of my foot and around the heel. The wood didn't bend and my feet hurt all the time.

I struggled with the shoes, because when they got wet, my feet would stay cold. Both feet were frostbitten. The pain in my toes was worse when my toes started to warm up again, and I could hardly walk.

The cows were so big. When I first arrived at the farm I thought they were going to eat me. In order to fill the troughs with food for the cows, I needed to get past them inside the stalls. I learned to push their heads aside with both my hands, and they would move a little and allow me through. It took me a long time to learn how to milk a cow; they kept kicking at me and they were so much bigger. I grew a couple inches that first year, after that it was better for me.

The first harvest time while at the farm, Hartman had me help with cutting the hay. Horses pulled the hay cutter and I walked right behind it and every couple steps reached over the blade to pull the hay over and back into the blade. I used a rake. For some reason after a while, the horses slowed causing me to lose my footing and I fell. Hartman stopped the machine quickly and jumped off to check and while patting my leg, very anxiously said, "Is it hurting, is it hurting?" He was so scared I was hurt. After that I wasn't assigned to that task. He said, "You need to be stronger, Mazie" and I was so grateful not to do it anymore. Hartman called me, Mazie, slang for the word mädchen, which meant "girl".

Hartman tried to teach me how to slaughter a chicken, by holding the legs and putting down the wings, and then cutting the head off. But instead, I accidentally cut of the chicken's face, and it got loose and ran away. The exasperated farmer gave up teaching me. I also did the laundry and to bleach the sheets, laid them out onto the grass in the sun, and watered them down, over and over again. I worked very hard at it, but the geese would always come and mess them up. The old grandmother would just say, "Oh well, they're good enough." I proceeded to shake off the mess the geese made and brought the sheets into the house.

When I finished the laundry, I would get a pan of water once a week or sometimes longer, and brought the pan to my cubby to wash myself.

Once in a while, I helped the old grandmother dress in the morning by bringing her the clothes she planned to wear for the day. Carrying the heavy old style dress with its large gathered skirt was difficult for the feeble old woman. She would say, "Bring me my frock."

After about a year working the German farm, one of the SS brothers came home to visit his mother and brother. He arrived with his wife, who wore beautiful clothes, so colorful and modern, different from anything I ever saw before. While his wife visited in the house with his mother, the old grandmother, Umma, he strolled toward me while I worked in the yard. He extended his hand to shake mine, and asked where I was from. He told me he was stationed at Radom. When he said it, I felt an adrenalin rush. *Radom was near Sulejów.* I didn't tell him where I was from, because of the fear I had of the SS and all they stood for and there he was, looming over me in his black SS uniform, the devil himself! His insistence aggravated me, so I began answering "ja" or "nien" and pretended not to understand and kept saying, "Ich verstehen nicht" (I don't understand). Since it had been a years' time, I was conditioned not to respond to anyone with fear. By being thrust into imprisonment and living under oppression, void of a family's love, this brought out indifference in me. Living that way for so long, I believed I would never achieve adulthood and be in charge of my own life. Then sixteen years old, bitterness grew within me.

Grateful when the SS brother's wife called him into the house to eat, I stayed away from the areas nearby until after they left, and I was relieved not to see or speak with him again.

When "Umma" died, I had no emotional feeling about her even after I saw Hartman's sadness as he cried for his mother's loss. Other than that, I don't remember anything about her death or funeral. I worked and my conditioned indifference clung to me like a shroud of unconscious security. I kept myself intentionally detached because they were Germans and in my child's mind, all Germans were bad people. I knew that these people controlled my life.

As I stated earlier, I was expected to work whether I slept the night before or not. Working constantly, I observed life going on around me. The Germans in our locale were farmers and had families who lived their normal lives, but supporting my child's opinion of the German people there were two situations which remain in my memory. The first is how I saw two teenaged girls who walked by the farm regularly while I worked. I envied their walking so freely in their youth. After a while, they weren't there anymore. Having heard about them one day, I learned that they were sent away to be impregnated by German soldiers who were chosen as "perfect" to keep the German ideal of a pure race growing. When the girls were back walking by the farm, I watched them often and could tell they were happy this happened for them. I accepted the story to be true when their pregnancies progressed month-after-month.

The second remembrance is about younger boys that I would see around the town at the beginning of my incarceration when we were brought back and forth to the farm from the barracks where we slept at night. The boys just disappeared. There were little girls around, but no boys. What I understood, they were sent away to Nazi youth camps, and were called Hitler-Jugend, where they would grow up learning the Nazi concept being part of the growing regime. Of course, I don't really know if all the families willingly gave their sons to Hitler, but as young as I was and because I thought all Germans were bad people, these stories confirmed my belief.

CHAPTER 12
A CONSTANT

At the Hartman farm, not very far from the industrial places, where munitions were assembled, the sound of bombs exploding became part of everyday living. Trains collected in large railway centers, and bridges connected over rivers for trucks, cars and pedestrians, which attracted the allied forces. The impact of a bomb with the ground, shook under my feet, and over and over I heard the thunderous b-boom, b-boom, b-boom. After a while, I started not to notice when the ground trembled, until a later time when the bombings were less.

CHAPTER 13
LIVING LIBERATED

After my liberation and finding Lodzia, we ended up in a place where there were many people just like us. The American Military Government took charge. Displaced people, as we were, received food rations, blankets, and clothes, and if we got sick, the American military medical clinic was close by, where a nurse or medics helped us.

Many of us gathered together in the same area, and were placed in a large German Military Camp south of Sehlen near Gemünden. The camp, inside a very large underground bunker with trees and bushes growing above as camouflage, showed us all how well the German soldiers knew how to hide.

The war ended in Europe, June 5, 1945. Many of us did not know if any of our families survived the war. We all waited, hoping for eventual news. There was a large group of Polish people and of course, many other nationalities. Although we worked well altogether, just happy to be free again, we mostly divided into groupings by nationality because we were drawn to our own.

With small children as part of our new community, activities such as, school classes, sports, and recreation gave the children a new focus, so different than the horrifying existence they recently came out of. It took a while to get everything organized, but since food and other needs were supplied by the U.S. Army, we could take the time to get it done. Eventually we organized to do our own cooking, laundry, and many other things necessary for daily living. I even managed to remove the letter P (for Polish) from the front of my dress. Having the freedom to take care of ourselves was great!

CHAPTER 14
WHEN I MET FREDDIE

Sometime around May 1945, eight young Polish men came to the camp. I only heard about them at first, because eight men arriving together was big news and people talked about it.

I learned they had been prisoners of war in East Germany. That part of Germany would soon be occupied by the Russians. These young men took part in the 1944 Warsaw Uprising. They were captured when the Germans destroyed Warsaw completely.

General Eisenhower went about fifty miles farther than originally directed. The eight men were freed because the General went beyond the intended point; they were literally in the East German prison within those fifty extra miles.

The eight men did not want to get caught behind the lines again. General Eisenhower's army liberated them, but they understood that the Americans were moving back to the line originally intended in the Yalta Agreement. These eight men decided they'd had enough tyranny and they made the decision to travel west. Before the Russian forces came, they found a truck and started to drive. The truck broke down in the Frankfurt/Marburg area, near the displaced persons camp where Lodzia and I were living.

I met Freddie in a group with many people and after a while, he just kept hanging around me. He and his group of seven friends couldn't get truck parts, so they ended up staying at the camp. I didn't know how Freddie could even look at me. I was a mess; five of my teeth were broken. That happened when the German soldier hit me. After a while the enamel peeled off, and my teeth started to rot, probably from poor nutrition and limited good hygiene as I grew up. But in any case, Freddie and I just started to talk and got to know each other. There were two women; both named Barbara, who were also liberated by General Eisenhower about the same time as Freddie. They had not been imprisoned very long, but as everyone else, were very grateful to be free. I envied them because they were both beautiful and their teeth were in great condition, because of their short imprisonment. They both liked Freddie and I was sure he would be attracted to one of them. He kept close to me, though, every time we met up in the group. Freddie became very protective of me, and made sure other guys knew how he felt about me. His attentiveness, apparent to everyone we knew, was not discouraged by his brother, Charlie, with whom Freddie was very close. Now with Freddie and me together, everything changed. He protected me from everything. After a while, I didn't worry about the two Barbara's anymore. I became friends with them both.

Teresa and Freddie

1945

Freddie and his friends got stuck at the camp, because Freddie met me, and we fell in love. His brother, Charlie, along with the group of their six friends, after about three months' time, were ready to move farther west. I would not go with them because I would not leave Lodzia behind. Freddie said if Teresa won't leave, he'd never see her again, so he wouldn't go. Then Charlie said, he couldn't leave his little brother behind, *"what would his parents think?"* not that anybody knew if their parents were even alive. Freddie and Charlie did not go. The other six boys stayed, too. Summer went on. When all the people in the refugee camp started to split up to go home, go west, choose a new country or become a German subject, Lodzia decided to go back to Poland to find her son, Jurek. He was seven months old when we were arrested and she was eager to find him and see how he'd grown; Lodzia wanted to go home. Since we couldn't be sure if anyone was alive in our family, I decided to stay with Freddie. I didn't want to lose him and he was not going back to Poland. Lodzia stayed with me through the summer and in the area until early fall waiting for her paperwork to come through.

Just after Lodzia left for Poland, Freddie and his brother found an old maroon colored Mercedes

Benz in a dilapidated barn. The farmer who owned the barn couldn't fix it, so it meant nothing to him. He told us we could have the car if we got it off his property. Freddie, Charlie, and the other six friends from the East German Prison were clever and with their combined knowledge, they fixed the car, including major body rust. We all liked having access to the car, but had to be careful of gasoline. Since we rarely used it and we weren't far from Sehlen, where Patten liberated me, one day I said, "Let's go for a ride. We can go to the Hartman farm for a visit." Just to get away for an afternoon, we did. Charlie, and Jurek Zaleski, Freddie's friend from the uprising in Poland, went with us.

I shook Hartman's hand. "It's nice to see you," he said, "you look good." I could tell he was impressed with the car, "It must be very nice to ride in such a good automobile." He was kind to us and Freddie had a nice conversation with him, just like we were meeting for the first time. There was no animosity. He offered us cider to drink, but because I was afraid of how they prepared it, I refused. I felt sorry for Hartman.

Nothing had changed for him. The farmhouse was practically falling down and I thought it should have been condemned by that time. Jella was still there as a volunteer, but she didn't speak to us. She just stood far away and watched us from a distance. As I looked around, time encapsulated itself for me. I lived and worked there for two years, but now in my mind it all bunched together like it was one day. We only stayed a half an hour, but it gave me closure.

Shortly after that, even though Freddie tried to tell him not to, his friend, Jurek went back to Poland. He pleaded with his friend and explained over and over that he would be imprisoned by the Russians if he went back, because of their involvement with the resistance and with the 1944 Warsaw Uprising. "That's why Charlie and I are so strong about staying here or going farther west or to America; we want to stay away from the Russians." But, Jurek, intent to get back to his home, didn't listen.

CHAPTER 15
GETTING TO AMERICA

After the summer of 1945, more and more people were going back to their countries; the displaced persons camp was closed and dismantled. Freddie and I, and Charlie, too, moved to Marburg to emigrate.

People who could find a job, moved on. Four girls, the two Barbara's, Stephanie, and me, with Freddie and Charlie moved to Hoffstadt Strasse number 6. (This was the street where we found a room to live). We slept on the floor, on the couch and wherever we could, to make it all work in one room. Freddie and Charlie both got jobs at the American army base near Marburg. They both spoke English well enough to be able to function with the Americans.

The women only stayed with us about a month or so. One of the Barbara's needed medical attention, so the other Barbara went with her to a medical facility for her to get treatment. We never heard from them again. Stephanie left about the same time, and I don't remember where she went.

Lodzia did not move to Marburg with me. She stayed in the camp as it closed to get her papers ready to go back to Poland to find family and her son. She visited me in Marburg, but she mostly stayed close to where the Military Governor was located to be repatriated back to Poland. He was the one who handled displaced persons paperwork to go back to their home countries. She finally went back to Poland in October of 1945.

Freddie and I talked about getting married in

the future. Since Freddie and his brother had relatives in the U.S., they thought it would be a good idea to see if the three of us could emigrate together. But, I would not be allowed to go with them unless I married Freddie.

August 10, 1945 Freddie and I went to apply for a wedding license. We knew we needed to get a license, but nobody told us that getting a marriage license in Germany was the actual wedding ceremony. We just thought we'd get the license and later get married in church. I went to get the license with my hair in curlers and not dressed up. Freddie wasn't dressed up either. Lodzia didn't even come with us. We looked in the room and there were candles on the table with the judge all dressed up and the room decorated. I almost died of embarrassment. Quickly, I ran into another room close by and combed out my hair and made myself look the best I could, and that was that. A gramophone played music from the corner and the judge found a couple employees from the court house to be our witnesses. The way the witnesses spoke, these people did this for other couples, too. Sometimes, when I think about the different situations, there were…some funny moments.

We heard about an American Consulate to be opened in Frankfurt. Freddie and Charlie were familiar with the process to emigrate to the U.S. because their father worked in the American Embassy visa department in Warsaw before the war. With that knowledge they went to Frankfurt. There they found out that the consul wasn't there yet, but there was a man they could talk to. He was the temporary consul. The man, Cordell Hull, was the former U.S. Secretary of State, and the most amazing thing, he knew Freddie and Charlie! My guardian angel was hard at work again. Cordell Hull visited Warsaw during and before the war. He stayed with Freddie's folks, because during the occupation the American embassy in Warsaw was closed. Freddie's father was the only person with keys to the embassy; it was a great responsibility.

When Mr. Hull recognized them, he wanted to know how they got to Marburg and "where is your father?" Of course, they did not know.

Having relatives in the U.S. and also knowing Mr. Hull gave us an edge to get to the correct papers for emigrating. We needed to wait until May 1946 to get there, and would arrive not as displaced persons, but under the German emigration quota. This was a great advantage.

While we waited, Freddie, Charlie and I moved to 45 Wilhelm Strasse, just before our second wedding, a church ceremony, in December 1945. This house was owned by a couple, Kama and Zbygniew Wawrzyniecki. The Wawrzyniecki's had friends, a couple, Dr. and Mrs. Sznelle. After a while, we moved in with this couple. They were a Polish woman and a German man, good and caring people.

Freddie and I planned for our upcoming church wedding. When asked if we had rings for the ceremony, we said no. Mrs. Sznelle pulled a silver spoon from a drawer and handed it to me. We took the spoon to a jeweler. Our two wedding bands were made from the silver spoon so generously given to us by Dr. and Mrs. Sznelle.

We lived with them six to seven months. While we lived there, I conceived our first child and we still lived with them when he was born four months early and weighing only one and a half pounds. I didn't have enough strength to allow him to grow well, because my body was so depleted by malnutrition during my growth years through the extended six years of war time. The doctor's tried to help my premature son, but he was too small. To warm his little body, the hospital staff preheated bricks, and laid them next to him, but he was just too underdeveloped. He struggled for a few days and then died. I had no way to help him, just like my mother had no way to help me when the Germans took me away. We named him Chester after Freddie's father.

Freddie and I were the only two people at the cemetery. We bought the plot for as far into the future as allowed at that time, 30 years. Freddie carried the little white coffin; it was so nice and white. He died in February 1946.

A short time after Chester died, Dr. Sznelle, a dentist, appalled by the condition of my teeth, began to work on them. He spent two months pulling teeth, repairing others and building some bridges, but ran out of time, because our emigration paperwork came through. My teeth were finally finished by an American dentist a couple years later.

On May 11, 1946 we left Germany after great preparation through the consulate for entry into the U.S. We had all the detailed and correct paperwork. Freddie was so excited; he knew when we were in America, opportunity knew no boundaries; there would be a way to succeed, no matter what. I loved Freddie and he was now my family. I didn't know if anyone other than Lodzia survived back in Poland, for me, choosing a future with a flicker of hope was right. We sailed on the S.S. Marine Flasher out of Bremerhaven, Germany.

Passenger Manifest from the SS Marine Flasher, shows Alfred Lejman, Teresa Lejman (wife), and Kasimiers Lejmanski (brother Charlie).

The rough crossing brought seasickness for me the whole trip. Freddie and Charlie felt great all the way. Finally, the last day, a sailor suggested to me to go to the back of the ship and look away to the horizon. This action helped me a little.

Practically the whole trip I contemplated my future and wondered if I did the right thing by moving to a strange new country. I didn't speak any English which concerned me about transitioning.

The ship arrived in the New York harbor at night, so I didn't really see the Statue of Liberty. I hadn't thought much about it, especially with all the crew's announcements to get ready to debark and being hurried along through each step of getting ashore. I'd heard about the Statue of Liberty, but knew more about the Eiffel Tower in France.

No one met us in New York as our paperwork was so perfectly organized. We could travel all the way to Flint, Michigan, to meet the family which was contacted by the consulate before we left Germany. Fella Rozoff, Freddie and Charlie's aunt, met us at the train in Flint. The three of us initially stayed with her, their Dad's sister, and her husband, Thomas. We were also in touch with John Gido, an uncle, Vickie Pandur, an aunt, all on Freddie and Charlie's side of the family. After a while, we moved in with John Gido's father and his second wife who lived next door. We occupied a couple rooms upstairs, very much like half an apartment. Charlie lived with us. He slept on the couch in the living room. We lived there a couple years and while there, I worked on learning English. I read a poem in the newspaper, liked it and cut it out for myself to read over and over again. Practicing this poem helped me to build a familiarity with English phrasing.

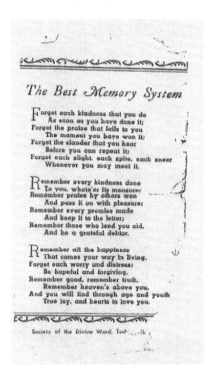

While still living with the Gido's, our first daughter was born in Flint's Hurley Hospital. My English, still not good, created a difficulty when speaking with hospital employees. I planned to name our first daughter, Krystyna Irma Lejman. Krystyna spelled the Polish way, and Irma, because I heard a radio show called, *My Friend Irma*. I never heard the name Irma before and liked it. But when the information was written down for me, the hospital staff person wrote Irma Christina Lejman, backwards and the wrong spelling.

CHAPTER 16
FINALLY ON OUR OWN

Charlie heard about an opportunity to sell Kirby vacuum cleaners door-to-door, and convinced Freddie to partner this venture with him. Freddie believed strongly that opportunity was right around the corner, even though his high school and early college major's paperwork for chemistry and physics, was lost to him. With no papers to back up all the courses taken, he never pursued those fields again. To take on the new idea promoted by Charlie, we moved to Detroit. The short-lived endeavor proved to be unsuccessful and Charlie soon after, moved back to Flint. Freddie tried a little longer, hopeful to be able to support me and our new child, but when no one bought vacuum cleaners from him, he tried to find other jobs.

He made friends easily where ever he went, and one of those friendships, opened a door to have access to a camera shop's dark room. The proprietor allowed Freddie to develop his own pictures, and he had the chance to be part of a group of people who had similar interests and to learn more about cameras. None of these were paid jobs, but Freddie was always working to open doors for himself and support our family.

Freddie in photographer's studio

Freddie's ID for working with local photographers.

No worthwhile work available, we eventually moved back to Flint, too. Again, we stayed with family, Aunt Fella Rozof, for a short period of time. Freddie got a job at the new Flint Chevrolet assembly line, and we found our own apt. We lived on Hamilton Street about a year, and while there, our second daughter was born in Flint's St. Joseph Hospital.

While in the hospital after the birth, I heard a song on the radio from the Broadway Production, *Where's Charley?* The song, *Once in Love with Amy*, sung by Ray Bolger, gave me another American name I'd never heard before. The middle name I chose came from the wife of one of Aunt Fella's son's, Bernie Rozof. Her name was Elaine. The couple was very good to Freddie and I. We named our second daughter, Amy Elaine Lejman.

We found a deal for property in Swartz Creek on Elms Road. No down payment was necessary; it was a land contract directly from the owners and consisted of a chicken coop, and nine acres of land, for $10-a-month. Eventually, Freddie built the chicken coop into a house so we could live on our land. There was still an outhouse as a bathroom, but soon after we drilled a well to get water inside the house. We lived there three years.

While there and after working at Chevrolet for about one year, Freddie had an accident in the plant while he stood high up on "the line". Falling backwards off scaffolding, landing on a rail right in the middle of his back, kept him in the hospital for about five weeks, and in a body cast for six months. After that, he was able to wear a special body cast only at night to help with the extended recovery time. To exist through those tough times, we lived off the disability payments Freddie received from Chevrolet. We had no knowledge of how insurance worked, having received no advice from the union and sadly just didn't understand our rights at that time for such an extreme circumstance.

I didn't have a driver's license and needed to drive. Freddie wouldn't be able to for a long time. I had driven before, but very rarely and I never had a driver's license. While at the DMV I told the clerk, "I drove in Germany, before we came to this country." My tone in my broken English rang true; the clerk issued me a license with no test. I learned the rules later, but at least I could "technically" drive legally to get to the store for food and get Freddie to the doctor for follow-up visits and for the many physical therapy sessions to get him back to be a functional person again. I did what I needed to do; my survival instinct kicked in again.

The owners of the chicken coop introduced another opportunity to Freddie and me. We needed to move to Bridgeport, a small town about forty miles north of Swartz Creek, to run a group of cabins. We would live in an apartment home above a cleaning business next door to the new business. Freddie was easily convinced, because he felt it was making progress in our lives. The life taking care of the cabins was very hard, renting, cleaning and keeping up the property. I managed to accomplish all the cleaning needs for the cabins and did not like this challenge, but after the experience of constant cleaning and taking care of myself during war-time, I made this new "calling" look easy.

While working at the cabin rental business, Freddie started to work as a carpenter for a local contractor in the Saginaw area. He worked and he studied carpentry and eventually received his own carpenter's license. After three years working with the cabins in Bridgeport, Freddie worked out another deal for an even-exchange for a house in the Highland Park School area of Saginaw County for the property with the cabins. During that time, the schools in the Highland Park area were suffering from diminished ratings, as school systems go, so Freddie and I placed Irma into a parochial school nearby. She needed a higher level of learning, because the students at her level in Highland Park were far behind the levels which Irma had already accomplished. Irma suffered terribly during that year, because of her difficulty in adjusting to the parochial system. For Amy, in Kindergarten at that time, the experience in Highland Park had minimal affect. She basically played in school for half a school year.

After only one year and to get back to a better school district for Irma and Amy, Bridgeport to be specific, Freddie worked out an even exchange for a brand new house on Pine Street. This "deal" through a co-worker carpenter friend, Marvin Deneau, helped grow Freddie's network in the contracting industry.

A few years later the telephone rang while Freddie was at work and the girls were in school. I answered normally, of course, not knowing who was calling. I said, "Hello" and waited for whoever they were to say something. I said, "Hello" over and over, but the caller didn't say anything. Just when I was about to hang up, I heard this little voice, "Hello,

Mom?"

"Amy, is that you, why didn't you answer me when I said hello?"

"I'm sorry Mom; I didn't recognize your voice. I never knew you had an accent."

"What are you talking about? I sound like I always have."

"Mom, really, I never knew you had an accent." I thought this was very strange, especially when she told me later, from the telephone call and onward she then heard my accent, but never prior to that time. Since arriving in the United States before she was born and speaking only English to her since birth, Amy somehow never differentiated the tone in my voice with the Polish accent. Amy was ten years old and I'd been in this country fifteen years.

CHAPTER 17
OVERVIEW

Freddie and I knew our life would be good; however, in the beginning, life in the U.S. was very hard. I did not speak English, which made it impossible for me to get a job. Life's circumstances constantly changed. Irma was born February 1947. Three years later Amy was born.

In 1948, through the International Red Cross, I found my family in Poland, and we began to communicate through letters for the first time. Shortly after that, Freddie found his parents. Working together with Charlie, they were able to bring their parents over.

They eventually settled in Toronto, Ontario, Canada.

As the years went on we became "American" living well-rounded lives within our communities. I learned to speak English, but I was not a very good speller, having never attended any kind of American school or classes. Self-educated, as time went by, proudly, I became a United States citizen in 1964.

CHAPTER 18
JAN AND MARCIANNA LESKI, MY FATHER AND MOTHER

I learned that the Gestapo arrested my mother, Marcianna Leska, about a year after the soldiers incarcerated Lodzia and me. She, also, transported in box/cattle cars, endured the same filth and degradation thrust onto us when Lodzia and I were arrested. At one point when the boxcar door closed, my mother's thumb got caught as it slammed shut. She screamed and screamed for the Gestapo to open the door, but they didn't. Almost two days she stood in agony with her thumb trapped by the sealed door. Finally, when the door opened, the other prisoners helped her. All that was left was dead tissue for half her thumb.

They sent Mom to the concentration camp at Ravensbrück. This experimentation camp used their Polish political prisoners as test subjects for medical research. The Germans used Mom's legs to test anti-frost-bite medicines. Just before the liberation army's came through, she was released to the International Red Cross and sent to Sweden for her extended recovery. Her legs, very damaged from the experimentation, took a long time to heal. Unconscious for an extended period, when she awoke, nuns who were nurses took care of her and they spoke a language she didn't understand. Mom thought she was in heaven.

My guardian angel found Mom in Sweden. Even with the horrible experiments to her legs, Mom survived.

During all this time I did not know where my father and my Aunt Mary were. They did survive the war. The day the Gestapo arrested Mom, Aunt Mary took Lodzia's little boy, Jurek, with her and ran away to the woods where they lived out the war together with the underground partisans. Jurek, kept quiet for so long during those years, he didn't learn to talk until he was three years old. I believe my dad also hid with the same groups of underground sympathizers as Aunt Mary and Jurek. They constantly moved between groups for safety. When my dad came home, not needing to hide any longer, as the patriot he was, he began serving his community right away. It was during the time when so many of the exiled Polish leaders were still transitioning back to Poland and our cities needed leadership. Dad was appointed Mayor of Sulejów.

Because of the extended period of war, six years, teenagers and young adults were conditioned to being non-productive and disillusioned. Dad organized the young people to set up a large barn as a place to make baskets out of the reeds that grew along the banks of the Pilica River running through Sulejów. These reeds grew in the sandbars close to the water's edge and were very pliable. Between forty and sixty people worked with him making baskets; this helped bring them out of their depression. They became productive people, selling their creations and then shipping them out as a business venture. (I didn't learn these facts until I was able to communicate with my family again.)

CHAPTER 19
ALFRED W. LEJMAN
(FREDDIE)

Early in 1960, at age 34, Freddie got very sick. Diagnosed with Hodgkin's disease, he endured newly introduced drugs pre-chemotherapy and extended hospital stays in two different facilities.

At first, three months in St. Mary's Hospital, Saginaw, Michigan and when they needed better diagnosticians, they transported him by ambulance the three hour ride to Henry Ford Hospital in Detroit. The many months traveling back and forth to see Freddie on weekends, a very expensive endeavor paying for gasoline and food for the girls and I, wore heavily on me. Driving so late on Friday nights, I was distracted and frantic to get there. Sitting on the passenger side of the front seat, I saw in Irma's face, she could tell how anxious I was to get there safe. The elevator door opened and the dreary green walls with the metallic rods extending dimly lit bulbs from the ceiling tried to suck us up into the sad atmospheres of the hospitals at the time. It gave the girls and I the depressive feeling we knew Freddie felt every day during the week being without us. But Freddie's smiling face when we walked through the door or when we ran to greet him as he waited in the hallway for us, was so worth the effort and put the green ugly walls out of our thoughts.

While I spoke to the doctors and nursing staff, Amy laid on the bed with her dad as he helped her with math homework. He tickled her and then teased her about her tennis shoes squeaking a specific way in the hospital hallways, making her giggle. He said, "I can always tell it's you coming to see me, scurrying and squeaking on the tile floor." The anguish and heartache brought on during the long months of hospitalization disappeared with the shared weekend moments and brought our warm family feeling back to life.

Because the hospital was so far away and expensive on so many levels, I needed to work, being the sole bread winner at the time. I managed to get a second job, working at a baby clothes outlet, making the clothes in their small factory. It was called Dapper Doo and it was right in our little town of Bridgeport. I continued driving at my school bus job, working for the Bridgeport School System, which I got a few years before. The Polish friends Freddie and I met in the Detroit area, through family and in our early years in the states, sheltered the girls and me on weekends. Thank God for friends!

Once diagnosed, the Henry Ford Hospital literally paid for Freddie's treatment by absorbing the massive expense into the funding received by the hospital for cancer research and treatment. The new medicines they wanted to try were so exorbitantly priced and basically still almost considered experimental, that he had to sign some papers stating he allowed the doctors to "treat" his illness in that way.

After the treatment he came home, very weakened. The doctors gave me medications for Freddie to take, and when I asked what to do when we ran out; they just said not to worry about that. I knew the medicine costs were extremely high and more than we could pay for ongoing. I accepted that he was being sent home to die, so we wouldn't need more. Home a very short time, Freddie died December 3rd, 1961. Irma was fourteen years old and Amy, eleven. Sadly, he never got to meet my parents or my sister Sabina, my dream since I first met him.

His funeral procession was the largest I'd ever seen. Mixed together with the huge group of American friends Freddie had, were our wonderful Polish friends from Detroit and Flint. When they drove up to Bridgeport for the funeral, they brought a small bag of soil from Poland to place inside Freddie's casket. A gesture of the strong bond he had as a Polish Patriot who fought so gallantly with the Resistance fighters for his beloved Warsaw home and his new Polish American friends.

His professional friendships were many in the Saginaw and Bridgeport communities. The contractor bills which lay unpaid while Freddie was laid-up and so sick were withdrawn by many of the men he worked with as a contractor. Even when I had to place our beautiful old farmhouse up for sale, the doctor who treated Freddie, purchased it, getting it off the market fairly fast. The monies from the sale were used to pay remaining bills and allowed the girls and I to move into a tiny house closer to the village of Bridgeport.

My parents wanted me to pack up the girls and return to Poland. Since Freddie and I worked so hard for our American life, that idea made me feel like I would be turning my back on all our hopes and dreams. It would be so difficult for Irma and Amy to fit in and learn a language that, neither Freddie nor I taught them, because we wanted them to be American. There were so many decisions and choices to be made. Those were very dark times in my life, but my guardian angel watched over me once again.

CHAPTER 20
A NEW LIFE AGAIN

Not long after, I found someone willing to take on two almost grown children, and a wife. His name was Max Thomas and I grew to love him when he helped me with my automatic camera left with me after Freddie died. Having practiced the Catholic faith with Freddie and the girls, I struggled with the idea that Max was protestant and a divorced man. The very kind priest, who knew my family for so many years already, helped me. He gave me clarity so simplified by the common sense he practiced in his life as a good priest. He said, "As a practicing Catholic priest, following all the doctrines I live by, I can't condone your relationship with a divorced man. However, I've known Max as a member of our community for many years. I know his reputation, and that he is a good and kind man. I know he will be good to you and your daughters." The comfort of his words given in warmth of a true friend helped me to transition myself.

I began going to church with Max. At the time he attended the Bridgeport Community Church. I had never been to a protestant service before. It was during one of those services that I heard the hymn, *Onward Christian Soldiers*. I had never heard it before that time and the first words tore me up...*Onward Christian soldiers marching as to war*...those crusaders...why are we honoring soldiers going into battle to kill people? These words rang in my ears reliving the Germans marching into our house and ripping me away from my mother and my life as a child. To this day it holds distaste and anger for me. I hate it.

A few months later, Max and I were married. He had one daughter, Carol, from a previous marriage.

Max and I had two more daughters, Melissa and Marcianna. That makes five kid's altogether.

CHAPTER 21
MY FIRST TRIP TO POLAND

With my American citizenship intact, I traveled to Poland to see my family for the first time in the summer of 1965. The momentous reunion lasted through long days running together in endless conversations. The warm feelings of family were sublime.

Marcianna, Teresa and Jan Leski

There were many stories which brought me closure. One specifically explained what happened to our German neighbor who brought the Gestapo to our door the first time, so long before. He spied on many families, which gave the Germans reasons to imprison or kill our neighbors. After a period of time, it was apparently very obvious to the neighborhood who endangered so many lives over and over again. When the war was over, the neighbors apprehended the man and together they tied his legs with a long chain. They lowered him up-side-down into a local well and drowned him. Eventually, the well was covered over and a new well was dug. Local justice prevailed.

I visited Janina, my very best friend from childhood. She still lived in Sulejów and married a local farmer; together they raised very large horses. Her farm was very near the cemetery where she and I played together as children. The visit was joyous with all the perfect and happy reminiscences from before the war, but the most distinctive part of our visit had to do with our conversation about memory. The familiarity we felt toward each other jumped right back during this visit; however, we were both astounded by the gap in time from 1943 until then in 1965. We spoke so matter-of-fact of our current lives, relating to each other about our homes, husbands, and children. "How could this be? Weren't we just together yesterday?" Again proof of human capacity to not just live, but succeed in our lives. Upon my leaving, Janina grabbed a handcrafted crystal vase which sat on the window above her kitchen sink. "Here Terenia, please take this home with you to the United States. I want you to have something of mine." This, the first piece of crystal which started my huge collection, holds the perfect memory of a lifetime friendship.

During this first trip back to Poland, Lodzia and I, went to visit Jurek Zaleski, Freddie's friend from the 1944 Warsaw Uprising. As Freddie feared and never knew for sure, when Jurek got back to Poland in late 1945, the Russians imprisoned him. There he stayed for ten years. Jurek told me, "Day after day I sat in my cell and thought to myself, I should have listened to Freddie and Charlie."

Dr. Kwapiński, our neighbor who was taken to Auschwitz, worked in his capacity as a physician for the prisoners during his own imprisonment. During that same time, Sabina was also incarcerated at Auschwitz. After a while, Sabina heard about him. Over and over again, she tried to slip him a note through a guard/medic, "My name is Sabina Leska, I hope you remember me from Sulejów…" to give to the doctor, requesting some medicine to help her knees which were getting progressively worse as she lifted objects and shivered with the cold in the winter. Finally, one time, after two weeks' waiting and hoping, the medic brought an injection back for Sabina. She was thrilled and the injection made a huge difference in how her knees felt so she could work every day, the only way she knew to survive.

Later, when the German guards found out about a plot to cause problems for their jailers by the prisoners within the camp, they questioned him. The doctor would not give the Germans any names or information that he may have heard. After these interrogations, Dr. Kwapiński, killed himself, rather than be interrogated again, so that he would not give information to hurt any of his fellow prisoners. My neighbor from the beautiful villa up the hill was a major hero for the Polish people. The building where he had his medical clinic in Sulejów was not destroyed in the war and still stands today. A special placard placed on the building acknowledging his commitment to the Polish people was dedicated recently honoring his memory.

I spent lots of time talking to my sister, Sabina. The miracle that she actually survived Auschwitz happened about three months before her liberation. Sabina learned early in her imprisonment that there were different classifications of prisoners, Jewish, religious and political. She was categorized as a political hostage and was put to work with that group. As long as she could work and be productive, she was a benefit to the Germans. Used for making soup, her main job was collecting and bundling nettles in the nearby mountains low meadows where they grew prevalent. Carrying the huge bundles on her back was physically very hard work.

When there was a typhus outbreak in the camp, Sabina got sick, and after a while, she could not work anymore. Since she was no longer useful to the Germans, she was stripped of her clothing and kept naked with other prisoners, who were sick and stripped of their clothing, too. So ill, she was sure she would be put to death like so many others every day. Almost unconscious with no will to live anymore, the woman next to her said, "Sabina that's your number, raise your hand" as an orderly read from a list. After she managed to raise her hand, he finished reading, "Move to the side," the female orderly said.

When they followed the guard away, Sabina didn't understand where they were being led. She asked the orderly, "Where are we being taken?"

The orderly said, "They've decided not to burn Aryans today."

Placed in a different barrack with prisoners not as sick, she was given clothing and food. After that she got better and was able to stand and went back to work so she could stay alive. The woman, who told Sabina to raise her hand, saved her life. My guardian angel reached far.

What I learned about from Sabina and want to acknowledge are the scores and scores of people classified in the other categories, like religious and Jewish, who were automatically put to death every day by the Nazi's. They had no chance to survive after they were taken hostage. Their stories, documented by the tens-of-thousands, honor their individual lives after the World War II holocaust.

When I learned more and more about all the

sad tales of survival and loss upon my return to Poland, I deeply regretted not keeping a journal of my day-to-day experiences. Torn from my childhood and my family, there was no thought about remembering the bad times; it simply did not occur to me. As an adult, I still didn't want to talk about what happened to me, and when my family and children started to press me with questions about my history, I knew that many of my memories of the experiences of World War II were lost in my subconscious.

After many long talks with my sisters and my parents, my six week visit came to a close. Just before I boarded the plane to return to my American family, my father said, "You are now the head of a branch of our family in a new country. Make me proud."

Sabina and Teresa 2008

Made in the USA
Charleston, SC
18 December 2015